Space Ships

by
David Orme

Thunderbolts

Space Ships
by David Orme

Illustrated by Dylan Gibson

Published by Ransom Publishing Ltd.
Radley House, 8 St. Cross Road, Winchester, Hants. SO23 9HX, UK
www.ransom.co.uk

ISBN   978 178127 066 0
First published in 2013
Copyright © 2013 Ransom Publishing Ltd.

Illustrations copyright © 2013 Dylan Gibson
'Get the Facts' section - images copyright: cover, prelims, passim – Bertrand Benoit, Patrick McCracken, NASA; pp 6/7 - Gregory R Todd, NASA; pp 8/9 - NASA; pp 10/11 - NASA; pp 12/13 - NASA; pp 14/15 - NASA; pp 16/17 - European Space Agency, NASA; pp 18/19 - NASA; pp 20/21 - Bertrand Benoit, rfwil, NASA; pp 22/23 - NASA, Tony Lyons; p 36 - NASA.

A CIP catalogue record of this book is available from the British Library.

All rights reserved. No part of this publication may be reproduced, stored in a retrieval system, or transmitted, in any form or by any means, electronic, mechanical, photocopying, recording or otherwise, without the prior permission of the publishers.

The rights of David Orme to be identified as the author and of Dylan Gibson to be identified as the illustrator of this Work have been asserted by them in accordance with sections 77 and 78 of the Copyright, Design and Patents Act 1988.

Contents

Space Ships: The Facts   5

Mission to Mars   25

Space Ships: The Facts

Into space!

Sputnik 1 – first satellite.
October 1957.

The Apollo programme

On the Moon, 1971.

Buzz Aldrin – Apollo 11, 1969.

Moon buggy.
Apollo 17, 1972.

Space shuttle

32nd launch of space shuttle Atlantis, 2010.

10

'Discovery' in space.

Final landing of space shuttle Discovery, 2011.

Space stations

ISS, 2000

Skylab, 1973

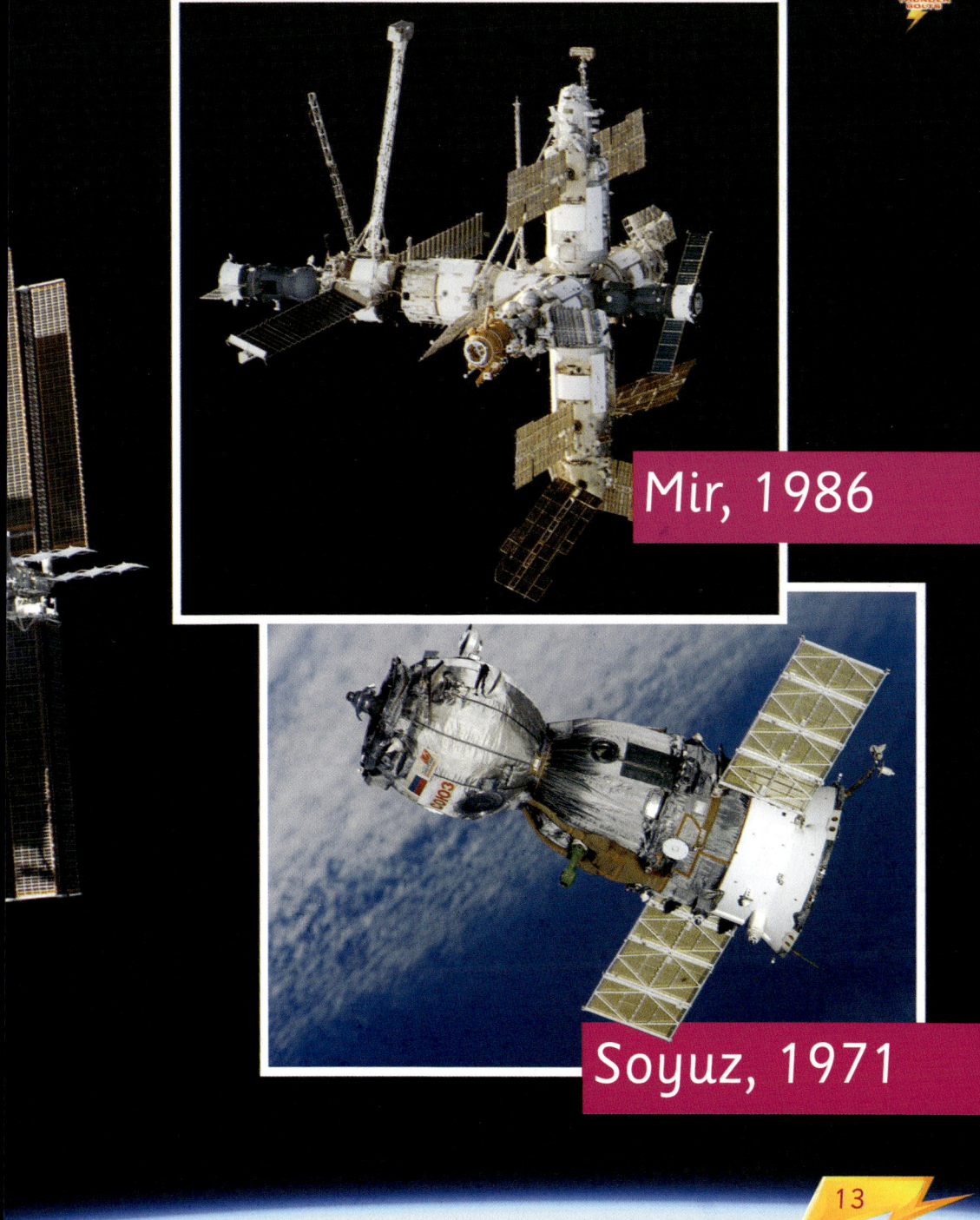

Mir, 1986

Soyuz, 1971

Voyager 2

Voyager 2 was sent out to visit the planets.

It is now more than 15 billion km from Earth.

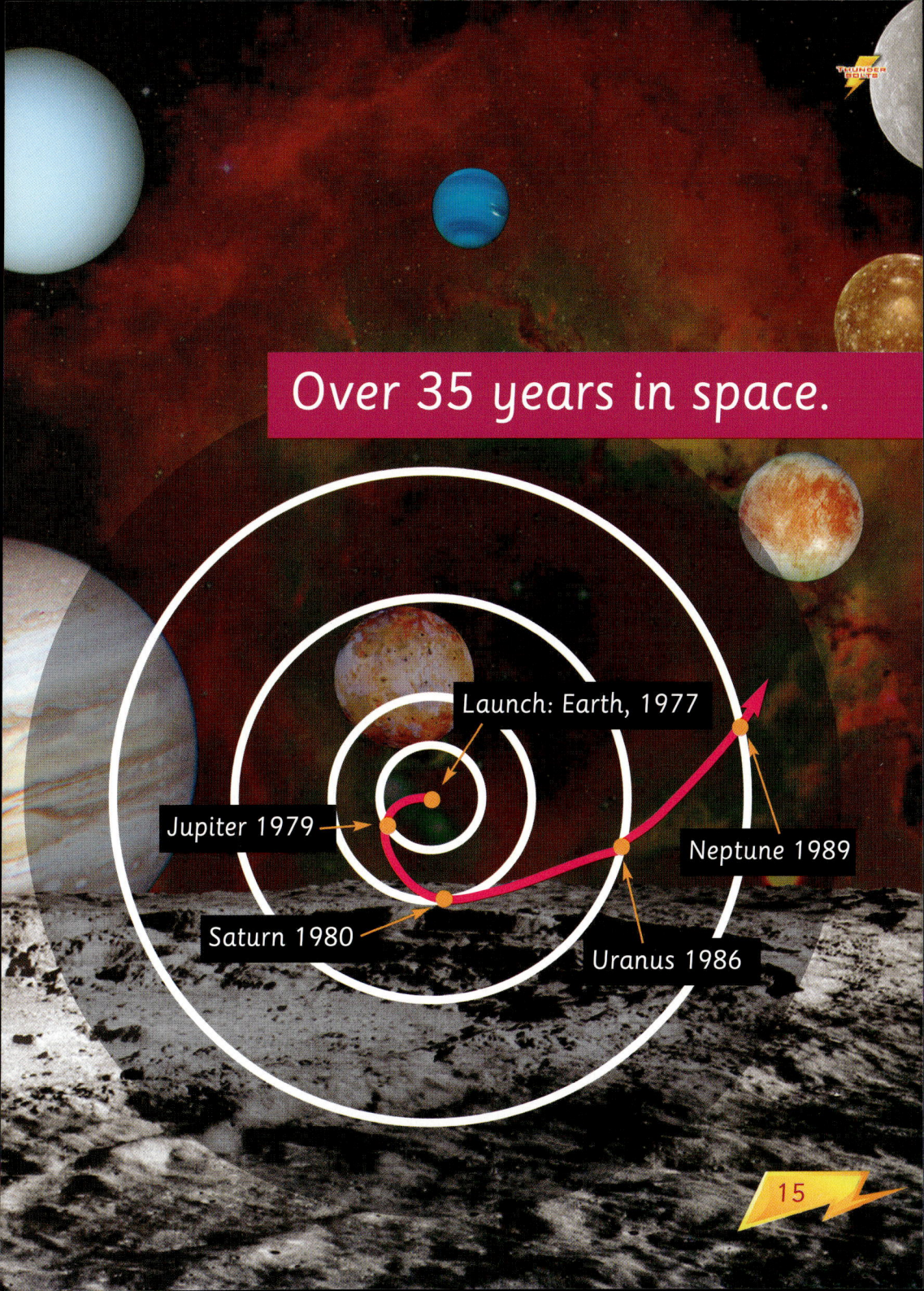

No. It was just a test.

Life on a space ship

'I can see Earth.'

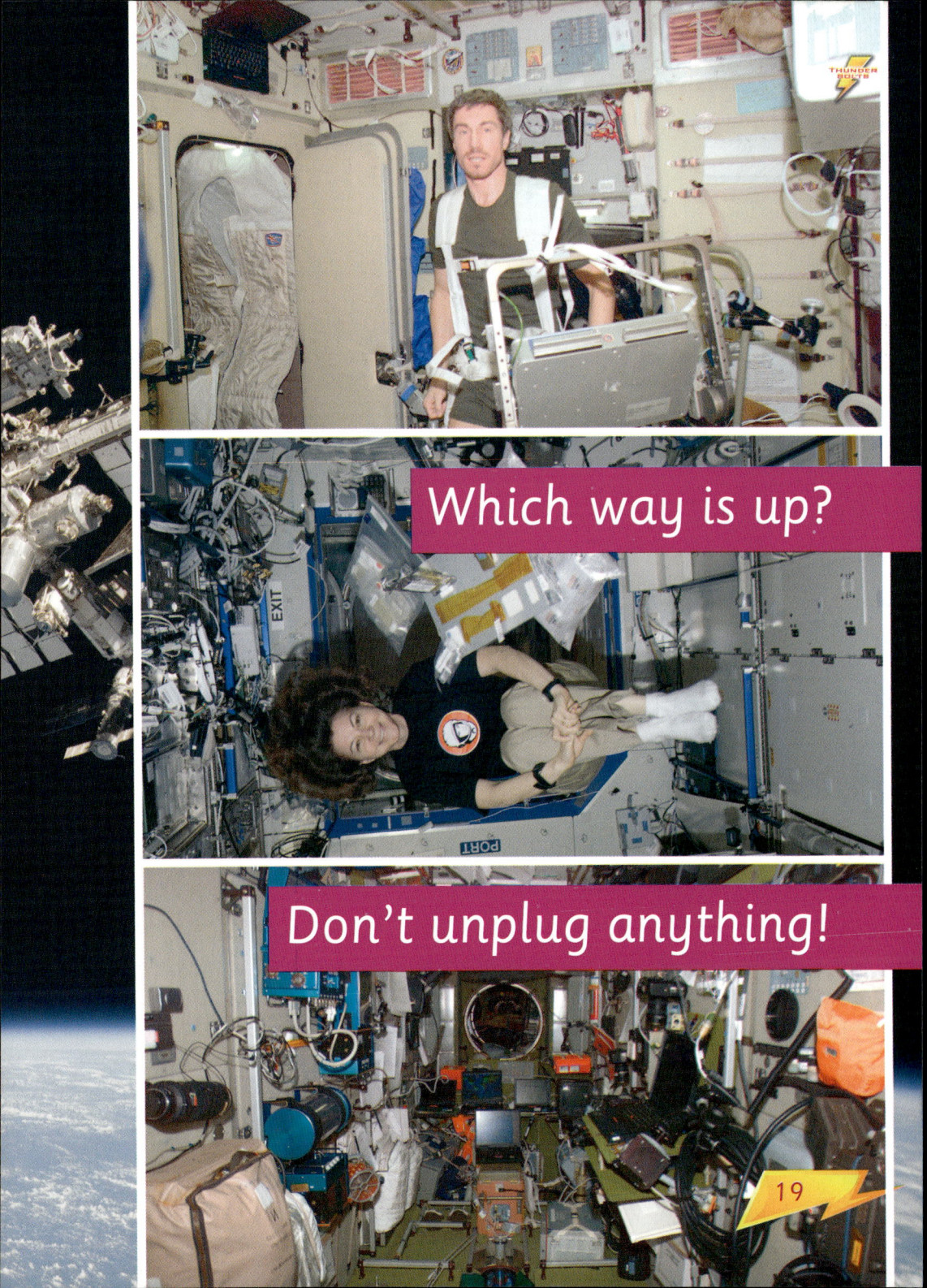

Which way is up?

Don't unplug anything!

Amazing space ships

Going to the stars

Will we ever get there?

What do you think?

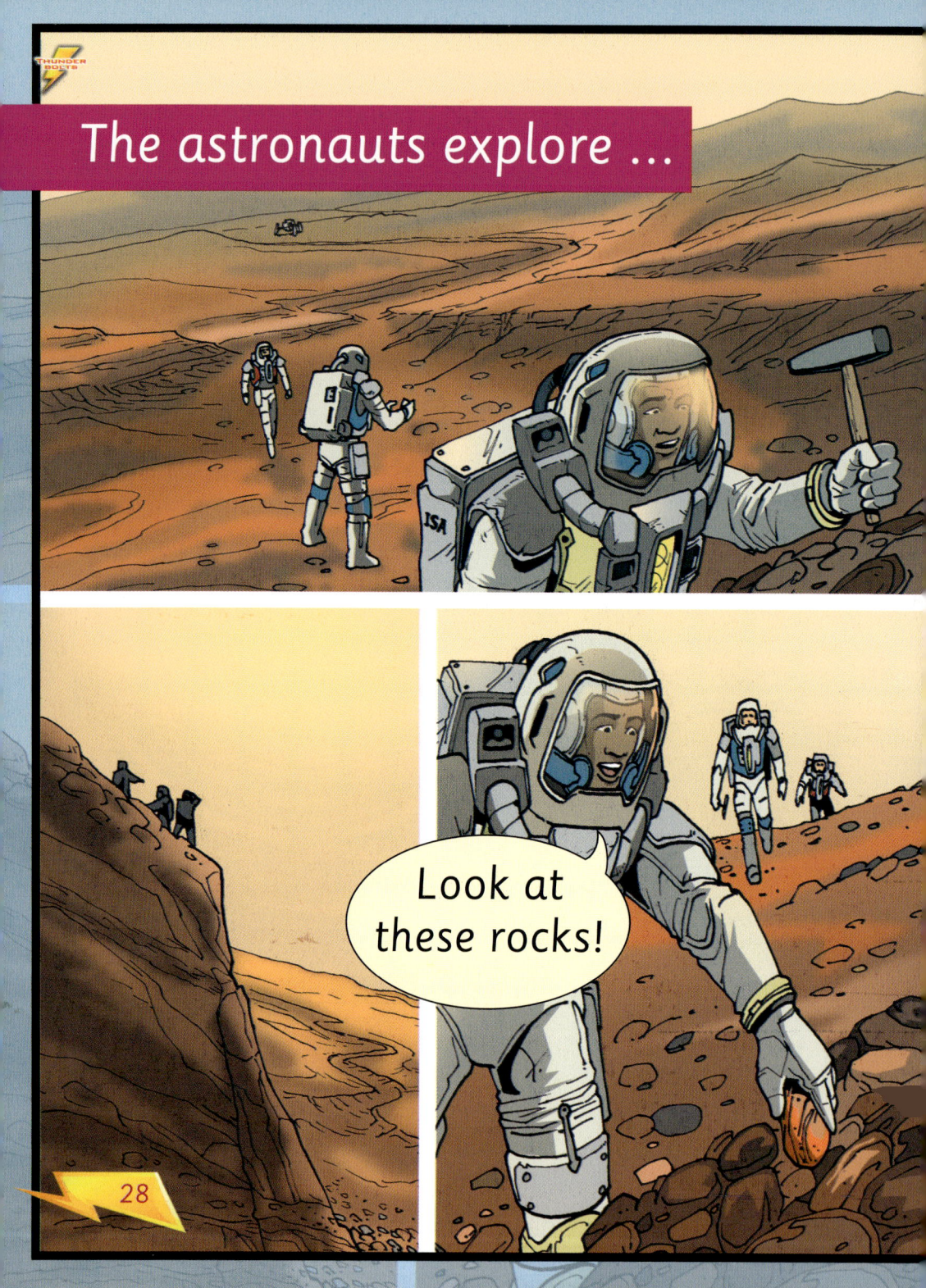

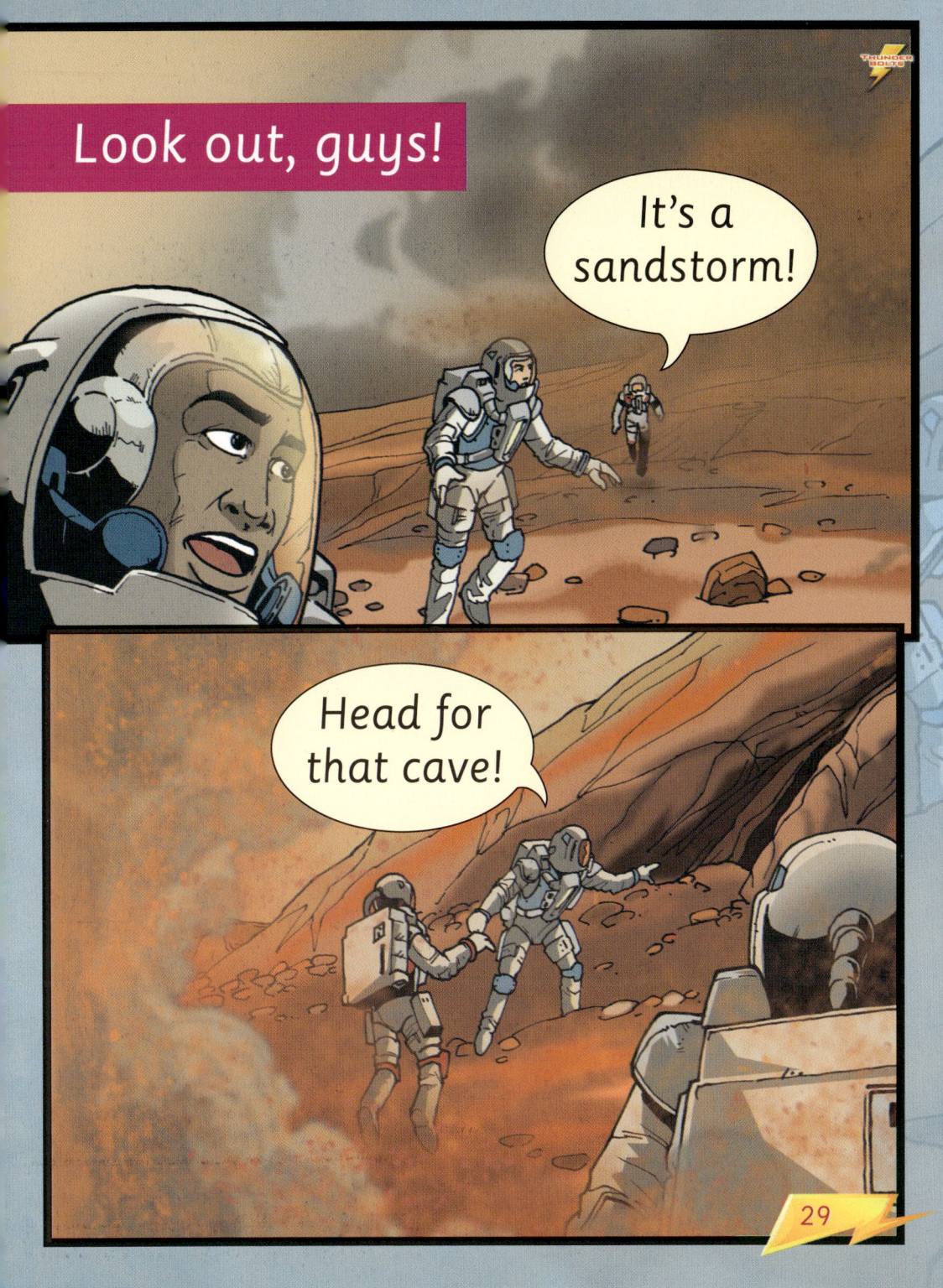

Word list

alien
Apollo
astronaut
billion
dust storm
Earth
Jupiter
launch
Mars
Moon

Moon buggy
Neptune
planet
satellite
Saturn
space shuttle
Sputnik
stars
Uranus
Vostok